1 0 0
GOLFING
TIPS

100 GOLFING TIPS

RICHARD BRADBEER · IAN MORRISON

SHOOTING STAR PRESS

A QUANTUM BOOK

Published by Shooting Star Press, Inc.
230 Fifth Avenue, Suite 1212
New York, NY 10001
USA

ISBN 1-57335-317-5

This book was produced by
Quantum Books Ltd
6 Blundell Street
London N7 9BH

Creative Director: Peter Bridgewater
Art Director: Ian Hunt
Designer: Stuart Walden
Project Editor: Shaun Barrington
Photographer: Ian Howes

Typeset in Great Britain by
Central Southern Typesetters, Eastbourne
Manufactured in Hong Kong by
Regent Publishing Services Limited
Printed in Singapore by
Star Standard Industries (Pte) Ltd

Directional instructions
throughout assume that the
player is right-handed.

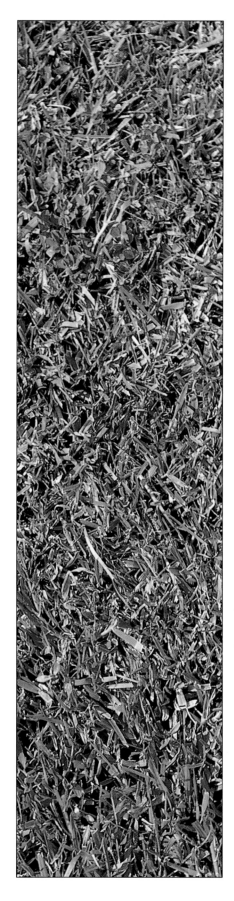

ᐧ ᐧ ᐧ ᐧ
CONTENTS
ᐧ ᐧ ᐧ ᐧ ᐧ

1

THE DEMANDS OF GOLF

There are many people who believe that golf is a good form of exercise and is a way of keeping you fit. Certainly it will not do you any harm, but in order to play good golf you need to be fit in the first place. In fact, physical fitness is only one of the demands the game of golf puts on you. The others are the *mental* and *enviromental* demands.

Golf needs intense concentration; that is one of the mental demands. It can also be a frustrating game at times. That is another mental demand. You should be ready for both during the course of a game.

Golf is a great 'leveller'. Because of the handicapping system, golfers of different standards can compete on level terms. If you are a low handicap player you are expected to win a lot. But if for some reason you are suddenly not winning regularly, then you have to cope with the situation. Probably you will need to go back to something elementary, like your hold, or stance, or swing. But being able to look for faults is proof that you can cope with the enviromental demands of the game.

2

WARMING UP: 1

You should never go into any sporting exercise without first warming up. A cold body will not respond well and that principle also applies to golf.

While you are waiting on the tee, or before you reach the teeing ground, do a couple of limbering up exercises to get the blood flowing through the muscles you are about to use.

Simulated golf swings with one, two or even three clubs in your hand, will certainly help as will the exercise shown, which will help to loosen up your back muscles and improve suppleness.

If you were a sprinter, or footballer, you would make sure you were warmed up before you raced or started your game. Golf is no different.

Place the club across your shoulder blades, holding it in place with your arms

Now complete a full turn of the body in the backswing

RIGHT Swing back rhythmically and gently to the follow-through position

6

. . . .

UNDERSTANDING AIM

. . . .

Many players, escpecially novices, will often believe they are aiming their club and ball in the correct direction when, in reality, it is either too far to the right, or left, of the target.

You must firstly identify the ball-to-target line, which is the imaginary line drawn between your ball and the target. Your feet should then be in line with that imaginary line and the leading edge of your club should be square to the ball and the line.

To establish the ball-to-target line, stand directly behind your ball and draw that imaginary line in your mind. Try picking out a landmark about 10ft in front of your ball which is in line between the ball and target, and use that as a guide for establishing your correct ball-to-target line.

The red flag is the target here. Check your body alignment by setting one club across the line of your toes and aiming at the target. Place another just inside the ball, parallel with the first club. Set another club between your feet, just inside your left heel with the grip just reaching the ball. This must be at right angles to the target line

7
CHECKING YOUR AIM

Aim, like hold, is one of the basics of golf. Get your grip wrong and you are going to encounter all sorts of problems. And if you don't aim in the right direction, then, how can you realistically expect the ball to go where you want it?

It is surprising how many novice golfers think they are aiming in the right direction. But when you analyze their aim, it is well off-target.

To appreciate aim, you must first understand what is meant by the ball-to-target line. Draw an imaginary line from your ball to its intended target, whether it be a flagstick or some point on the fairway, that imaginary line is the ball-to-target line. To aim correctly, the leading edge of your club should be at right angles to the ball and ball-to-target line. If it is, then your aim is correct.

After setting your club in position on the ground, visually check by looking between the clubhead and target a couple of times to make sure your aim is correct. Don't take it for granted that your aim is correct, even the best players don't do that. You should constantly check your aim. Any slight error will cause the ball to veer away from its intended target.

Watch the flight of your ball to see what your regular flight path is. You can then allow for this when you take aim

8
UNDERSTANDING BALL FLIGHT

Ball flight is simply what it says and describes the flight the golf ball takes after you hit it. The **straight** flight does, as its name implies, see the ball travel in a straight line.

The scourge of the high-handicap golfer is either the **slice** or the **hook,** which are flight paths, arising from errors.

The slice sees the ball start its journey heading to the left then veering to the right. The hook is the opposite.

Two other flights are the **push** and **pull.** Like the slice and hook they go out to the right and left accordingly, but in both cases the ball doesn't start its travels by going the opposite way first.

Finally, the other two flight paths are the **draw** and **fade.** The former is a shot that sees the golf ball travel out to the right slightly before returning to the target. The fade is the opposite.

9

OPEN AND CLOSED CLUBHEADS

Every golf shot is made with the leading edge of the club square to the ball-to-target line. Don't forget that. Occasionally, you will hear commentators say; 'he played that with an open (or closed) club face'. The club face is *never* actually opened or closed. Your stance creates a so-called 'open' or 'closed' club face but contact is still with the **leading edge square to the ball-to-target line.**

A closed clubhead is one with the leading edge pointing to the left of the ball-to-target line, while an open clubhead points to the right of the ball-to-target line. The correct position should be square.

An open or closed club face will seriously affect the flight of the ball. The most common cause of the club face being opened or closed is because of an incorrect grip.

TOP LEFT This picture shows the open club face

ABOVE An open clubface

ABOVE The cubface here is already slightly closed. Imagine its position by the time it reaches the front ball

ABOVE A closed clubface

TOP LEFT This is the correct position of the club across the left hand

ABOVE View of the correct left hand hold from a chest-on viewpoint

10

· · · ·

THE HOLD – THE LEFT HAND

· · · ·

The hold, more commonly, but incorrectly, called the 'grip', is a crucial aspect of golf. Get the hold wrong and you can expect all sorts of problems.

The left hand is the most dominant of the two hands when adopting your hold, but you do not grip the club with all four fingers and thumb of the hand. Only the first three fingers are used.

To grip the club correctly place the club diagonally across the palm of your left hand and apply pressure with the first three fingers. The thumb and index finger are to be used for support only; not for gripping the handle of the club.

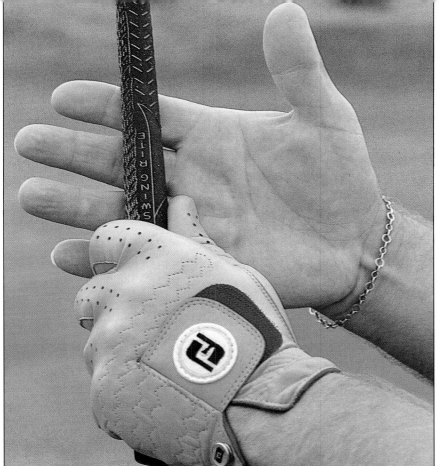

TOP LEFT The 'V's' formed by the index finger and thumb of both hands point midway between head and right shoulder

TOP RIGHT How the club should lie across the right hand

11

· · · ·

THE HOLD – THE RIGHT HAND

· · · ·

Having correctly placed the club in the left hand, now place the right hand on the club but apply pressure with the second and third fingers only. All other fingers are for support. You should adopt any one of the three standard holds. Each is designed to accommodate hands of various shapes and sizes. The grips are so designed for personal comfort, no other reason. Why not try all three to see how comfortable (or uncomfortable) you feel with each? There will be one to suit your needs.

Irrespective of which hold you adopt, you must make sure that your hands are kept as close together as possible and that the little finger of your left hand is approximately one inch from the top of the handle. It is also important that both your hands work together as one unit.

To check that you are holding the club correctly, place the club-head on the floor in the address position. The 'V's formed by the index finger and thumb of each hand should *both* be pointing to a point midway between your head and right shoulder. This rule applies no matter which club you are using. If you are having problems with your swing at any time, check your hold, it could be that's where your problems are starting.

12
. . . .
ADOPTING THE OVERLAPPING HOLD
. . . .

Commonly referred to as the Vardon grip, the overlapping hold is named after the six-times winner of the British Open, Harry Vardon, who is widely reported to have been the first man to use it. It is regarded as the standard hold and is the most popular of the three holds.

The little finger of your right hand (if you are right-handed) rests on top of the forefinger of your left hand.

It is important with the overlapping hold, and with other types of holds mentioned for full shots that the 'V' formed by the thumb and forefinger of each hand points in the same direction, ie to a point between your face and right shoulder.

13
. . . .
ADOPTING THE INTERLOCKING HOLD
. . . .

The interlocking grip is very little different to the overlapping hold, but this time the forefinger of the gloved hand and the little finger of your right hand overlap. This grip is ideal for lady golfers or male players with small hands.

BOTTOM LEFT The overlapping hold

BOTTOM RIGHT The interlocking hold

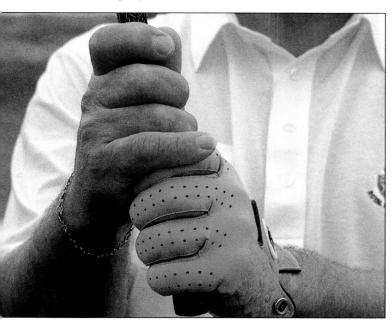

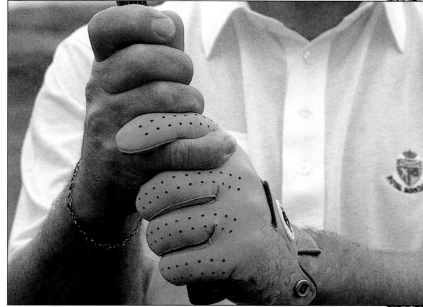

ABOVE The two-handed hold, with every finger on the handle

FAR RIGHT A relaxed address position. There should be no feeling of tension

14

ADOPTING THE TWO-HANDED HOLD

This is the least used of all holds but is one adopted by people who are unable to put a strong hold on the handle. As you will see, all your fingers and thumbs come into contact with the club handle. It is similar to the hold a baseball player would have on his bat. It is also sometimes referred to as the double-handed grip.

15

ADDRESSING THE BALL

The ball position in relation to your feet is important. For woods and longer irons it should be level with your left heel. But as the club gets shorter then the position of the ball moves to a point midway between your two feet.

To make sure your address is correct, line up the leading edge of your club with the ball and ball-to-target line. Then adopt your normal hold. You should now be in the correct address position.

16

RELAX AT ADDRESS

Many golfers, as soon as they stand on the tee and address the ball, suddenly feel a tenseness run through their body. This happens to the novice quite often on the first tee when there is a great deal of pressure on him to 'get the ball away'. A tense body does nothing for the smooth rhythm of the swing.

The tension often starts in the hands and spreads throughout the body. Check that you are not gripping the club too tightly. You need a firm, but not over-tight, grip. If you are conscious that you are gripping too tightly then let go of the club, step back from the ball, and start all over again. It is amazing just how much this can help.

17
· · · ·
POSITIONING THE BALL IN RELATION TO YOUR FEET
· · · ·

When playing a shot, the position of the ball will be dictated by the length of club being used. When using a driver, for example, the ball will be positioned at a point level with your left heel. But as the club gets shorter, to say a 9-iron, the ball position will move away from your left foot to a position between your two feet.

18
· · · ·
HOW HIGH TO TEE THE BALL
· · · ·

The only advice on this subject is to make sure that, with woods, at least half the ball is visible over the top of the club face at address. But don't tee it up too high. The size of the club face will therefore dictate how high you tee-up your ball.

You wouldn't tee the ball this high when using an iron club off the tee. In fact, you don't have to tee your ball on a teeing peg. At

TOP LEFT Ball position for the driver

ABOVE For a 9-iron, the ball is further back, almost to the midway point between the feet

RIGHT About half the ball is visible above the face of this wooden club

short holes the more experienced golfers prefer to play the ball off the ground so as to improve the chance of imparting backspin on the ball. However, as a matter of etiquette, and so as not to cause damage to the teeing ground, you are advised to use a teeing peg at all times.

Don't forget, you aren't allowed to tee up your ball on the fairway, only on the teeing ground. In winter months most courses allow 'preferred lies' to protect the course, but this doesn't mean you can take out a tee and tee up your ball!

TOP LEFT Bend forward from the hips for the address position. Your knees should only bend enough to avoid stiffness

ABOVE A chest-on view of the address position

19
· · · ·
THE CORRECT POSTURE
· · · ·

One of the biggest faults of the high-handicap player is the bending of his, or her, knees too much.

The most important thing to remember about correct posture is adopting the correct angle of your spine. To establish this, stand upright and bend your back slightly forward so that your hips and rear-end stick out just slightly. Then flex your knees inward towards each other.

You must maintain this spinal angle throughout your golf swing.

ABOVE When you hold your left arm straight down your side, the club forms an angle

TOP RIGHT At address there isn't a straight line between club and arm to the shoulder

20
· · · ·
SETTING THE CORRECT LEFT ARM POSITION
· · · ·

Many novices think the left arm and club have to be straight as one unit. This is not the case. Try holding your left arm straight down by your side and put a club in your hand and try to maintain it as one straight unit. The only way you can do so is by tilting your body to the right. That is not a natural stance for anything, let alone playing golf.

You must keep your left arm straight when swinging a golf club but to appreciate what this really means, hold your arm down by your side and open your fingers slightly and insert any club. You will now see that the club is at an angle. You will also see that your left arm *is* straight. That is the correct and natural way to hold a golf club. When you adopt your stance at address you should maintain that hold, don't try to make the point between the clubhead and your shoulder one continuous line.

If you look at the handle of your club you will note a pattern. This is there to help you to ensure your hands are lined up with the leading edge.

21
· · · ·
THE INCORRECT LEFT ARM POSITION
· · · ·

See what happens when the left arm is kept straight and rigid? The left arm is elevated far too much and the entire body looks tense. When we say 'keep a straight left arm' it means at the top of the back swing, *not* in the address position.

22
· · · ·
SHOULDER POSITION AT THE ADDRESS
· · · ·

Having adopted a good posture with a perfect spinal angle you will now be in such a position that you can make at least a complete 90° shoulder turn, which is crucial to the full golf shot. When you take up your correct address your right shoulder should be slightly lower than your left.

If you turn your shoulders through a complete 90°, your hips will turn through 45°.

ABOVE The head is slightly behind the ball

BELOW The head remains in the same position at the top of the backswing. It shouldn't be pulled further to your right

BOTTOM RIGHT The head is still behind the ball just after impact

23

HEAD POSITION AT THE ADDRESS

Except when putting, when your head is directly over the ball, it should at all other times be slightly behind the ball. If it is not, then you are stretching, which means your swing will be unbalanced and consequently a whole host of problems are in store. So, keep your head *slightly* behind the ball.

24

HEAD POSITION – IN THE BACKSWING AND AT IMPACT

Note how, throughout the swing the head remains in the same position at the backswing and even at impact is still behind the ball. This is a very important point to remember when playing the golf shot, keep your head behind the ball.

25

YOUR WRISTS: THE SHORT GAME

In most golf shots your wrists 'cock' as part of the stroke. The point of the backswing when they actually 'cock' depends upon the club being used.

When playing the short game, ie when using the short irons, then they cock earlier than with the long irons or woods.

BELOW LEFT Early wrist cock when playing a short iron

ABOVE With a long iron, the wrists should cock much later

26

YOUR WRISTS: THE LONG GAME

With long irons and woods the wrists don't cock until nearly at the top of the back swing. The simple rule to remember is: the shorter the club, the earlier the wrists 'cock'.

30

UNDERSTANDING SWING PATH

The entire left side of the body moves to the right in one piece

Firstly you must understand what is meant by **Outside** and **Inside.**

If you adopt your normal stance your feet are positioned on the **Inside** of the ball-to-target line. The area the other side of the line is known as **Outside.**

A normal golf stroke is played with an **inside-to-square** swing path. In other words, the clubhead is taken back on the inside, makes contact with the ball, and follows through on the inside.

A swing that sees the clubhead taken away on the outside and follows through on the inside, after making contact, is known as the **out-to-in** swing path. And a clubhead taken away on the inside and following through on the outside is known as an **in-to-out** swing path.

Remember these three swing paths: we will come across them quite a lot when looking at faults and their causes later on. Often problems are caused by an incorrect swing path.

31

THE TAKEAWAY

The takeaway is the first action in the golf swing. So make sure you get it right. If you don't then you cannot expect the clubhead to be in the right place at impact.

It is a one-piece movement and the entire left side of your body, including the shaft and clubhead, move towards your right side. This is all made possible because your right hip and shoulder move backward slightly.

However, it is important to make sure your hands and wrist maintain their shape and that your elbows remain a constant distance apart throughout the takeaway and the rest of the swing.

We said earlier that the leading edge must be square to the ball and ball-to-target line, and indeed it will be as you address the ball. But as you begin the takeaway it will no longer be square to the ball-to-target line. Don't worry, if you carry out the rest of the swing correctly it will be square when it returns to its impact position.

32
· · · ·
THE BACKSWING
· · · ·

TOP LEFT The left arm is comfortably – not rigidly – straight

ABOVE The clubhead has crossed the target line

FACING PAGE, TOP LEFT The club is in a flat, or laid-off position

FACING PAGE, TOP RIGHT The club is parallel with the target line

It is so important that after a smooth takeaway you now take the club into its backswing with a fluent and continuous movement of your upper body as your arms take the club above your head.

The backswing depends upon so many factors: you should make sure your wrists 'cock' naturally and that you keep your left arm straight. It doesn't have to be rigidly straight. It must, however, be comfortable.

At the top of the backswing your right elbow should be pointing at the ground slightly behind your right heel and the shaft of the club should be parallel to the ball-to-target line. And finally, you should have maintained you elbows at the same distance apart throughout the backswing; they should be the same distance apart at the top of the backswing as they were at the address. The club should be parallel to the ball-to-target line at the top of the back swing and *not* across the line or laid off.

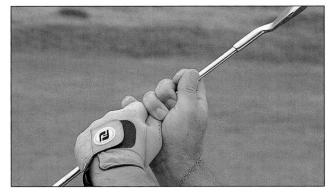

CENTRE LEFT Grip down the shaft to
see that your clubhead is reaching the correct
position at the top. This is fine, with the toe of the
club pointing towards the target

CENTRE RIGHT Here the clubface is shut

BOTTOM LEFT Now the clubface is open

33

THE DOWNSWING

From the top of your backswing you have now to bring the club back to its original position. This part of the swing is the downswing and is crucial.

Everything must come back down just as it went up, and in one complete unit. If it didn't then you can't expect your clubhead to be square to the ball and ball-to-target line at impact.

The hips play an important role in the downswing and they move slightly ahead of the hands as your weight is transferred to your left leg, enabling you to keep your body square at impact. It is important that you keep a steady head and maintain your correct spinal angle.

34
· · · ·
THE FOLLOW THROUGH
· · · ·

The action of the club following through will automatically bring your head up eventually, so don't be tempted to lift it early.

Once the clubhead has made contact with the ball, allow it to continue its swing so that it will end up behind your head. As it pulls upward after impact it will not only lift your head for you, but your weight will be transferred to your left leg and your right leg will be bent at the knee, with your right foot resting on the toe of your shoe.

35
· · · ·
CORRECT LEG POSITONS
· · · ·

At the top of the backswing your weight should be transferred to your right leg and your left knee bent inwards. On impact, the weight will have transferred to your left leg and your right knee will now be bent inward. As the swing is completed and you go into your follow-through position, your right knee will be pointing at the target and your right leg will be supported on your toes. The left foot will be slightly bent over onto its side.

Move your left foot nearer the target line in order
to close the stance

39
· · · ·
CLOSE YOUR STANCE WHEN
USING A WOOD
· · · ·

Because of the length of the wooden clubs and long irons, it is a good tip to adopt a slightly closed stance when playing a shot with one of these clubs.

With the club being longer you need to get your right shoulder out of the way during the swing. A slightly closed stance will help you to pivot better.

Playing with long irons – your shoulders should be level with the inside of your heels

40

. . . .

PLAYING WITH LONG IRONS

. . . .

You must appreciate that as club numbers get higher the length of the club gets shorter. Consequently it is impossible to adopt the same stance for every club. When you place a 1-iron on the ground you will notice how much flatter than a 9-iron it is. You have to make the necessary adjustment in your stance.

The long irons are those often referred to as the 1-, 2-, 3- and 4-irons. Because they are still regarded as the 'long clubs' you have to play them with a full swing just as you would if you were playing a wooden club. The ball position varies according to the length of club used. For a 1-iron it will be nearer to a point level with your left heel than with a 4-iron, when it moves to a position toward the midway point between your feet.

When adopting your stance for a long iron, your shoulder should be level with the inside of your heels. Your right foot should be slightly drawn back from the ball to target line, to enable you to get your body into a full swing.

41

· · · ·

PLAYING WITH MEDIUM IRONS

· · · ·

The medium irons are the 5, 6 and 7 irons. Because the length of the club is getting shorter then you should stand nearer to the ball at address and your shoulders should now be level with the outside of your heels.

Your feet, shoulders, knees and hips should now be square to the ball-to-target line. The right foot is not drawn back this time.

Because the club is shorter you adopt a more upright stance and as a result your swing is shorter.

As the ball position is now more towards the middle of your two feet, your head is not as far behind the ball as it was with the driver. But don't be tempted to move it forward; your head should still be behind the ball.

For the medium iron, the ball is further back in the stance and the body is again square to the ball-to-target line

When using the medium irons you are more likely to take divots with your shots; this is because of the upright nature of the swing. Divots are a natural part of the game. You are not doing anything wrong if you take a divot but, whatever you do, please replace the divot after you have played your shot.

42

PLAYING WITH SHORT IRONS

For a short pitch, the ball is almost opposite the right foot and the feet are close together

The short irons are the Nos. 8- and 9- irons and the two wedges, the pitching wedge and the sand wedge.

Take hold of a sand wedge and adopt your normal stance. Note where your hands are positioned. Now put it back in your bag and take out your driver and adopt your normal stance and again note where your hands are positioned. In both cases they should be in a position just above your left knee. If they aren't then you have adopted either the wrong hold or body position.

The purpose of this exercise is to show you how some things never change, no matter which club you are playing. All golf shots are the same, it's just that the clubs are of different length and different loft.

The ball position is now at a point midway between your two feet and your left foot should this time be drawn slightly back from the ball-to-target line. The reason for this is because the short iron shot is not played with a full swing, therefore you need to get your body out of the way quickly after making contact. Having your left foot drawn backward enables you to do so. When drawing the left foot back, make sure the shoulders do not move backward at the same time. They should still be parallel to the ball-to-target line.

43

OPEN YOUR STANCE WHEN PLAYING A SHORT IRON

Because you are not taking a full swing with the shorter irons, the left side of your body will not have time to get out the way as you pivot. Consequently, you need to adopt an open stance which will take your left side away early.

onto the safety of the fairway. If that is the best shot to play, then play it. That is ambition, not over-ambition.

When playing out of long grass, take a heavy club like a wedge. With your ball being buried in grass their will be a tendency for the club shaft to get wrapped up in the grass. Because the wedge has a heavy clubhead it will help make the path to the ball easier.

Take a more upright backswing so you are attacking the ball from an acute angle. Again, this will help to prevent the clubhead getting entangled in the grass. But the most important thing to remember is don't be too ambitious.

TOP LEFT Here the ball is well down in long grass. Use a lofted club to get out

TOP CENTRE Concentrate of making good ball contact

TOP RIGHT The player is well balanced here. He hasn't made the mistake of hitting flat out in the hope of greater distance

51
· · · ·
THE DIFFERENCE BETWEEN PITCHING AND CHIPPING
· · · ·

The **pitch** is played with a lofted club high into the air so that it lands on the green. Depending on the conditions of the ground and weather conditions, the ball may stop dead on landing or roll forward. It may even roll backward if a great deal of backspin has been imparted on the ball and/or conditions facilitate such a shot.

The **chip** is played with a less lofted club and the ball is chipped into the air before running on to its target.

52
. . . .
WHEN TO CHIP OR TO PITCH?
. . . .

Only you can make that decision. Obviously the lie of your ball and local conditions will help with your decision-making. If you are on the fairway with a steep bunker to an elevated green in front of you, then you are left with no alternative but to play the lofted pitch shot. But if you are just off the edge of the green with a clear run to the hole then a chip and run is your best shot. But you must always bear in mind conditions on the course. A wet fairway and green will lend itself to the pitch whereas a dry and rock-hard green is not the best surface to pitch to. In the latter case the chip would be better.

Don't forget also that wind affects the pitch because of the elevated loft of the ball. Lush grass is an ideal surface from which to pitch.

53
. . . .
PITCHING
. . . .

Pitching, like chipping, is that part of the game referred to as the short **game.** The pitch is played with a lofted club which projects the ball high into the air before landing on or near its intended target. It is a shot played with the hands and arms; a full rotation of the body is not necessary.

The key point to remember about pitching is to take less than a full swing of the club because the distance the ball travels is normally a short one.

You should adopt your normal hold on the club and make sure the leading edge is square to the ball and ball-to-target line. Make sure the ball is positioned slightly left of centre at address and keep your shoulders square to the ball-to-target line, but open your stance slightly by drawing back your left foot from the ball-to-target line.

You want to shift slightly more of your bodyweight on to your left leg than you would for a medium or long iron shot. As the downswing commences make sure even more weight is shifted to your left leg.

For delicate short pitch shots to the green move your hands

TOP The ball is well back in the stance. The descending blow will increase backspin

This is the length of swing needed for a short pitch

down the handle of the club to shorten it. For full pitches, hold the club near the top of the handle. Your follow through should be at least as long as your backswing. Finally, don't be afraid to use your sand wedge off the fairway.

54
· · · ·
GETTING THE BALL TO STOP AFTER PITCHING TO THE GREEN
· · · ·

Only the very best of players can get the ball to stop on pitching, but even they cannot do it all the time. A rock-hard green will not lend itself to such a shot, no matter how good the player is.

Top players can manipulate the ball by applying backspin but this requires the very best of contacts between club face and ball. Don't expect every one of your pitches to stop dead; they won't. You must remember that important word 'ambition' which we have used before. If you can pitch to the green and get yourself in a position for a single putt then you will have achieved your goal. Don't expect the ball to stop dead six inches from the hole every time.

TOP The ball is beginning to climb steeply

Weight is well over to the left side

55
· · · ·
A FINAL TIP ON PITCHING
· · · ·

A ball pitched to a green below your stance is more likely to stop than one pitched to a green above your stance.

56
· · · ·
CHIP AND RUN
· · · ·

The chip and run is played with a medium iron as opposed to the lofted club of the pitch. The ball is not played in such a lofted manner; it is only slightly lofted before landing and then running on to its intended target.

The leading edge should be square to the ball and ball-to-target line. Shorten the club slightly by moving your hands down the grip. You also want to take the loft off the club by holding your hands slightly forward at address. You want to open your stance and shift your bodyweight slightly on to your left leg.

57

· · · ·

WHERE TO AIM WHEN PITCHING AND CHIPPING

· · · ·

When chipping, a low running ball is the aim. De-loft the club by having the ball by the right heel and note that the take-away is one-piece. There should be little wrist break

When pitching it is advisable to use the flag as your aiming point. By doing this you are allowing for the ball, because of its trajectory, to drop into an area around the hole. When chipping, you want to use the hole as your aiming point.

58

REPAIRING PITCH MARKS AND DIVOTS

The divot is very much a part of some golf shots. Just because you take a divot with your shot doesn't mean you have played a bad stroke. However, if you do take a divot you must replace it and tread it back into its original place to give the grass a chance to grow again. If you see other divots which have not been replaced then don't leave them, put them back and play your part in maintaining the course.

It is obvious how much work goes into producing and maintaining the high quality of the putting surface. So, if your ball pitches onto the green, make sure you repair the pitch-mark with a pitch fork. And again, if you see somebody else's unrepaired pitch, then take the time to repair it.

Unlike when playing the pitch, the ball starts out with low flight

The follow-through is quite short because no more effort is being used than in putting

This is the so-called 'poached egg' lie. Think of sending both sand and ball out of the bunker

Out flies sand and ball

59

. . . .

PLAYING OUT OF A GREENSIDE BUNKER

. . . .

Before you enter the bunker, stand behind your ball and assess the shot you have to play. It is easier to get an idea of distance of your shot from outside the bunker than when you are stood in it.

A normal grip should be adopted when playing out of sand, but you should open your stance. Make sure your feet are comfortable in the sand and wriggle them into position before you address the ball, which should be positioned opposite your left heel. An open club face should be adopted.

Your shoulders should follow the line of your open stance and not be square to the ball-to-target line. Your backswing should be along the line of your shoulders and *not* along the line of the ball-to-target line. The backswing should be a wrist and arms action, and with a varying amount of body movement.

Concentrate your eyes on a position approximately 2in (5cm) behind the ball; it is this area the clubhead is going to strike.

There is a full follow-through. Don't just stop the clubhead in the sand. Instead, cut under the ball and go through with the shot

Because the club face is open, it travels under the sand and lifts the ball out of the bunker.

The amount of sand you take behind the ball depends on the distance the ball has to travel. The greater the distance, the less sand you take, and vice versa.

60

· · · ·

PLAYING FROM THE UPSLOPE OF THE BUNKER

· · · ·

Quite often, the big problem with this bunker shot is catching the lip of the trap with the ball. To overcome this problem you want to adopt a very open stance. However, it is equally important that you balance yourself well because one leg will be positioned higher than the other. Thereafter, the shot is very similar to playing the uphill lie off the fairway. Make sure you transfer plenty of weight onto your left leg.

A quick gain in height is needed to clear the lip of the bunker. Open your stance

From this plugged lie, the clubface is closed to help prevent it opening too far as it swings through the sand

The club is raised in a very upright path to avoid catching the back lip of the bunker

61

PLAYING A BALL PLUGGED IN SAND

This time you *don't* open your stance but play with a normal square stance, the ball positioned level with a point midway between your two feet.

The secret in getting the ball out of the sand now lies in playing a violent shot with a **closed** club face. The soft sand (it wouldn't have plugged if the sand was hard) will cause the clubface to open on impact.

You must try and create a follow through, but this depends upon the lie of the ball and how deeply it is plugged.

62

PLAYING FROM THE BACK OF THE BUNKER

Probably the worst type of bunker shot is the one with your ball at the very back of the bunker. There are two problems: firstly, you cannot get a good stance and secondly, the back of the bunker may hamper the clubhead in the back- and downswing.

You may have to stand with both feet outside the bunker or with one foot in, and the other out. Either way, you must create a very upright backswing to prevent the club hitting the back of the bunker. The upright backswing will create an open club face and it is important that you follow through after impact.

63

PLAYING OUT OF FAIRWAY BUNKERS

We have used the word 'ambition' several times before. But never is it as important as now, when you come to play a shot from a fairway bunker. How often does your ball seem to be sitting up nicely in the sand and with 150 yards to go to the green you optimistically take a 3-iron from your bag and hope to hit the

target, and what happens? The ball hits the lip of the bunker and drops back into the trap.

The actual stroke from a fairway bunker is not a difficult one, but you are well advised to take a club no stronger than a six- or seven-iron. You must always consider your next shot.

Make sure you have a firm hold, position your body square to the ball-to-target line (it doesn't need to be open this time) and focus your eyes on the ball, not the sand behind it, because this time you are playing the ball and not the sand.

64
. . . .
BUNKER ETIQUETTE
. . . .

When entering a bunker do so from the back of it and not the front. When you leave the bunker, make sure you rake over any footprints you may have left in the sand. If you don't then you are leaving footprints into which somebody else's ball can land. Don't forget you are not allowed to touch the sand with your club before playing your shot. If you do, you will be penalized two shots in stroke play and will lose the hole in matchplay.

The ball is against the centre of the clubface which is square with the line to the hole

65
. . . .
PUTTING BASICS
. . . .

The following are simple, but very important, basic principles of putting:

(1) Make sure you have a sound hold of the club

(2) Line your ball up square with the face of the putter and make sure it is in the centre of the club face

(3) Keep the club face at right angles to the ground and square to your point of aim

(4) Your eyes must be over the ball and your head must be still throughout the stroke

(5) Don't let your wrists break

Follow those simple guidelines and you are more than halfway toward becoming a good player on the putting surface. And don't forget: all putts are straight, it is the borrow and speed which determine the direction.

66

PUTTING: THE HOLD

The hold you adopt for the putting stroke is very different to your normal hold. The most popular hold these days is the **reverse overlap** but with a selection of 'big' putters being seen all the time, holds have to be manufactured to fit the clubs. We will deal with the conventional putter and the reverse overlap.

All your fingers and thumbs, with one exception, grip the club handle to make sure you have a firm hold which enables you to move the putter accurately.

The four fingers and thumb of your right hand should grip the handle, with the thumb on the flattened part of the handle. The first three fingers of your left hand also grip the handle and the thumb of this hand is also placed on the flattened part of the handle. The only finger which does not make contact with the handle is the index finger of your right hand. It rests along the tops of the fingers of your right hand . . . it has to go somewhere!

A good secure hold like this will not only aid the accurate movement of the putter but will prevent you cocking your wrists. The putting stroke is made with the shoulders, arms, and putter moving as one unit; it is not a 'wristy' stroke.

No wrist break with this putting stroke. It is a shoulder and arms movement

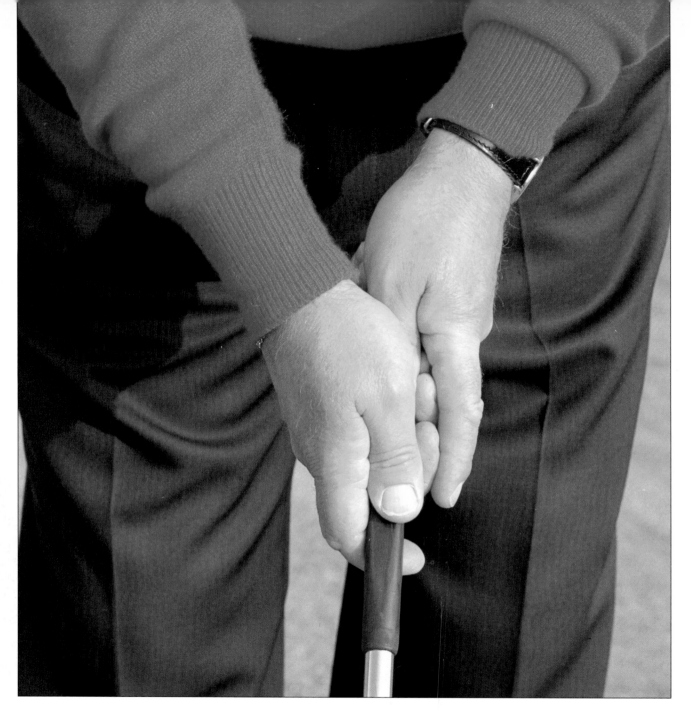

The reverse overlap putting hold seen first from in front of the player and then a chest-on view

67

· · · ·

BALL POSITION AT ADDRESS WHEN PUTTING

· · · ·

To encourage a top-spin strike of the ball, it should ideally be opposite your left foot at address, but this depends on your individual putting style. If you watch the professionals, you will see there is a wide variety in personal putting styles, but you are best to stick to the conventional putting method until you gain more confidence and are ready to experiment.

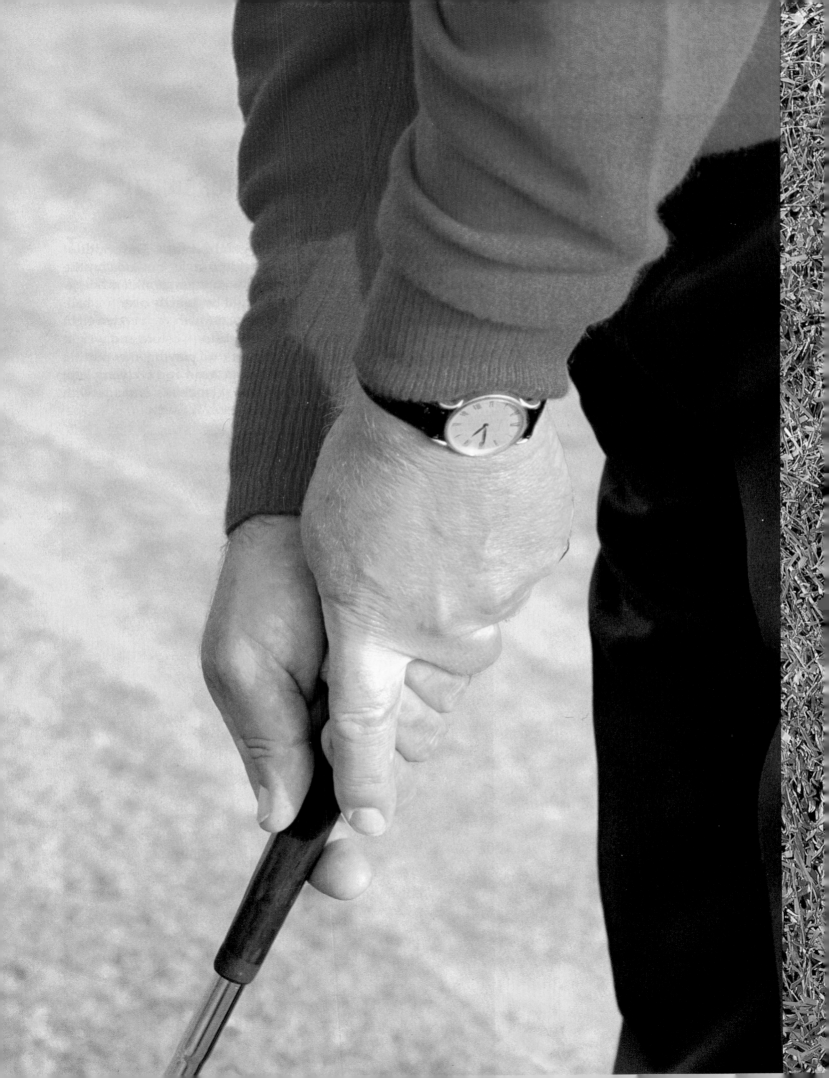

73

PREPARING FOR BAD WEATHER

Unlike cricket, rain doesn't stop play in golf. So you must be ready for the worst the elements can throw at you: or alternatively, you can go home! But that is a defeatist attitude.

You should make sure you always carry a good set of waterproofs in your golf bag, and have them ready to put on at the first sign of rain. But don't make the mistake, as so many people do, of putting the waterproofs on over your normal clothing without first taking essential items like tees, pencil, pitch forks, etc, out of your pockets. There is nothing more embarassing than having to take your waterproofs off again in order to get at these items.

Obviously, you will also need an umbrella to protect you in the rain; but the one thing many novice golfers ignore in adverse weather conditions is the **chill factor.** Make sure you keep yourself warm. There is nothing worse for your swing than a cold body and cold muscles. A spare sweater and a hat are useful additions to your golfing attire.

It is also useful to carry a towel in your bag and whatever you do, make sure you keep your hands dry and warm. Wet and cold hands will have a disastrous effect on your hold.

74

PLAYING IN WIND

You can't see the wind. It may not be there one minute, and the next it appears. It may be a headwind on one hole, or a side wind on another. Wind was invented to make the golfer's life a misery.

Unfortunately, you can never take on and beat the wind. But what you must do is make allowances for it. If you played a shot to a hole with, say, a 5-iron last week, but this week have a strong headwind on the same hole, then don't take the 5-iron again and expect to play the same shot: you must make allowances and take, perhaps, a 3-iron.

The wind won't only affect the flight of your ball, but will also throw your swing off balance if it is strong enough. To help your swing in windy conditions, move your hands an inch or two (2½–5cm) down the grip and compensate for this in your stance.

75
. . . .
PLAYING **WITH** THE **WIND**
. . . .

These conditions can be very advantageous to you becuse, with the wind behind you, your ball is going to travel further. For that reason, you must take a more lofted club than you would normally have taken. Only the strength of the wind and distance to the green will dictate your choice of club, but beware not to take a club with insufficient loft because if you do, the wind may carry your ball through the green and possibly into all sorts of trouble.

76
· · · ·
PLAYING INTO A HEADWIND
· · · ·

The opposite rules now apply. You want to take a less lofted club so that you keep your ball lower. If you take a club that is too lofted, then your ball will sail high into the air but won't travel far enough forward.

However, playing into a headwind when pitching to a green can be an advantage because you can, with the use of a lofted club, create a higher trajectory and therefore get the ball to hang in the air longer than usual before dropping onto its intended target.

77
· · ·
PLAYING IN A CROSSWIND
· · · ·

The left-to-right wind is regarded as the worst type of wind condition the right-handed player can play in. Obviously, the right-to-left wind is the worst for the left-handed player.

Because the wind is blowing at your back it will invariably throw you off balance. Consequently, you want to make sure you adopt a firm stance. Because of the strength of the wind your ball is going to be blown from the left to the right while in flight so you must aim sufficiently to the left to compensate. However, you *must* make sure you hit the ball straight and let the wind do the rest. If you slice or hook, or pull or push in such conditions, then you can expect a lot of problems. When playing with a right-to-left wind then you should this time aim your ball to the right of its target, and again make sure you hit it straight.

Waterproofs should not be too tight fitting, especially under the arms and across the shoulders

78

PLAYING IN RAIN

We have already told you about the merits of wearing good waterproofs and preparing yourself before you put them on. It is not often easy, but you should try and keep yourself as dry as possible. You should also ensure that you keep your clubs, particularly the grips, dry. You don't need to be told what can happen if you attempt to play a shot with a wet grip.

Also, make sure you keep your hands dry and if you are wearing a glove keep it protected while you are not playing a shot. You can buy all-weather gloves which don't absorb the rain as much as conventional leather ones. They are a wise investment.

Two other points to remember about playing in the rain: (1) The ground will be slippery, so make sure your shoes are well studded, and (2) Rainwater gathers on a golf ball. You are not allowed to dry your ball until it is on the putting surface. When playing from the fairway, the water will not go until the ball gets airborne. Therefore you want to get the ball airborne quicker than normal. The use of a slightly more lofted club will achieve this and probably not lose you any distance with your shot, because one will compensate for the other.

Ready to beat wind and rain

79

PLAYING IN THUNDER AND LIGHTNING

The best tip in such conditions is *get off the course*. However, if that is not immediately practicable, then these are two very important DONT'S.

(1) Don't put your umbrella up, unless you have a modern one with built-in safety measures.
(2) Don't shelter under a tree.

83
. . . .
CURING THE HOOK
. . . .

Like the slice, there are many possible causes of the hook. If it has crept into your game then look down this list; there is probably a cause which you can identify, and hopefully rectify.

(1) The biggest cause of the hook is having the leading edge turned inward at impact ie the club face is closed. Moving the hands too far forward at the address can cause the club face to become closed.

(2) You create an **in-to-out** swing path (see tip 30).

(3) At the top of the backswing the club has gone over the target line and is aiming to the right of the target.

(4) The right elbow is held too close to the body in the back-swing and downswing.

(5) A **strong** hold is adopted. In other words one or both hands are too far to the right on the grip.

(6) The shoulders are closed at address, often caused by having the ball positioned too far back.

Both hands here are in a very weak position

84
· · · ·
THE HOOK: AN INCORRECT HOLD
· · · ·

Unlike the slice, a strong hold is a probable cause of the hook. This time, one or both hands are too far to the right and not far enough around the handle.

A strong hold again. The ball is also too far back in the stance, causing the shoulders to be in a closed position

The hold on the club is now far too strong, sure cause of hooking

85

· · · ·

THE HOOK: INCORRECT BALL
POSITION AND ADDRESS

· · · ·

Positioning the ball too far back at address is one of the most common causes of the hook; because it is so far back there is a good chance that the club face will be closed at impact. While you are trying to get your head behind the ball, which is now too far back, you are distorting your body and it is no shape to manufacture an ideal golf swing. Closing the stance too much at address is also a possible cause of the hook.

86

· · · ·

TOPPING: THE CAUSES

· · · ·

A strong hold on the club causes the shoulders to look, and feel, cramped

Topping is that embarrassing shot which most novices make at some time. Proper contact is not made with the ball and it is hit toward the top. Consequently it doesn't get airborne. Newcomers to golf are under the impression the ball should be lifted into the air. It is not. The loft on the club is so designed to do that for you.

However, topping does happen. If it is happening to you then take a look at these possible causes:

(1) The ball is too far forward at address.

(2) If playing the ball off the tee it is not teed up high enough.

(3) You are standing too far away from the ball.

(4) Your head comes up at impact, normally caused by a poor weight distribution with your weight being transferred to your left leg on the backswing and to your right leg on the downswing.

(5) The collapsing of the left arm at the top of the backswing.

(6) Your hold on the club is too tight, causing a tension which results in the body being lifted at the moment of contact.

(7) Of course, playing with the wrong club can cause the ball to be topped. If your ball is plugged into a wet fairway then you wouldn't contemplate taking a driver out of your bag. You would use a medium or short iron.

87

FLUFFING: THE CAUSES

Fluffing is as embarassing to the novice golfer as topping. Fluffing occurs when the clubhead strikes the ground before making contact with the ball. It happens because the downswing is too steep and consequently so is the attack by the clubhead on the golf ball.

The most common cause of fluffing is having the ball positioned too far back at address. As a result your shoulders tilt and cause your arms to go too high in the air in the backswing and also transfer too much weight onto your left leg. If you let the club travel further than your body turns, then you will find yourself stabbing at the ball at impact and this will again cause fluffing.

88

RECOGNIZING FAULTS

It is easy to say; "I'm slicing because the club face is open at address". Indeed that is probably why you are slicing. But that is not the whole story. You have to find out *why* the club face is open at address and that may be because your right shoulder is turning too high, which causes the out-to-in swing path, which in turn causes your hands to be ahead of the ball at impact, opening the club face.

So it's no use identifying the obvious cause of the slice, or whatever error has crept into your game. You must go back and look at *all* the possible causes. Please remember *most faults can be found in the address position.* So use that as the starting point when looking for faults.

89

CONSIDERATION FOR OTHER GOLFERS

Golf can be a dangerous game if played negligently and without due consideration for other golfers out on the course. Be aware of

what is going on around you at all times. Don't play a shot until
the match in front of you is well out of range. However, if your
ball appears to be travelling in the direction of another player then
you must shout the acknowledged warning of 'fore!'.

Nothing but the best of manners is acceptable on the golf course
and the game should be played in the best spirit. Don't talk,
move, or make a noise while another player is about to play a
shot, and don't tee your ball up on the teeing ground until the
other players have taken their shot in the correct rotational order.

Don't waste time either. Get on with your game as quickly as
the match in front allows, and when you have putted out, don't
stand around discussing the hole with your playing partners.

90
. . . .
ALWAYS PLAY THE PROVISIONAL BALL
. . . .

If there is a chance that your ball will be lost, or may be out-of-
bounds, then you should always play a provisional ball. You will
not be penalized if your original ball is found and is playable. But
if it is not, then you have to go back to where the shot was played,
in order to try again, so you may as well play the provisional ball.
That is why the rules allow the playing of such a ball. However, if
your first ball isn't found, then you must play the provisional ball
from where it lies, under penalty.

91
. . . .
DROPPING YOUR BALL
. . . .

If you are forced to drop your ball because it is unplayable you
should first establish whether you are dropping under penalty or
not. But either way, you should know how to drop your ball
according to the rules.

Until recently it used to be dropped over the shoulder. But
these days the ball is dropped from arm's length and shoulder
height in front of you. The ball must be dropped as near to its
original position as possible but not *nearer* the hole. After dropping,
it must come to rest within two club-lengths of the point where it
first hit the ground. If this distance is in doubt and you have to
measure it, then use the longest club in your bag.

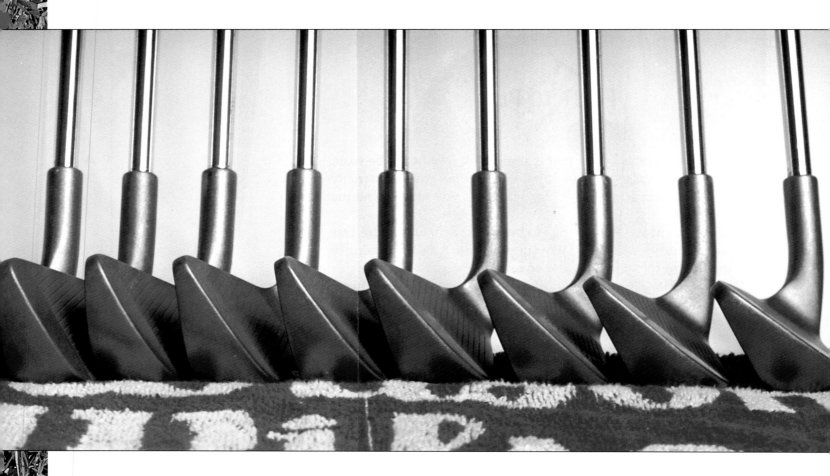

94

. . . .

LOOKING AFTER YOUR CLUBS

. . . .

They say a poor workman blames his tools. But if you allow your clubs to deteriorate then those 'tools' won't do the job properly for you, through your own fault.

You should always make sure the grooves on the club face are regularly cleaned out. They amass quite a lot of dirt during a round of golf and the grooves are not there just to gather dirt, they serve a purpose as an aid to the flight of the golf ball. Dirty grooves won't do their job properly. Furthermore, they will cause damage to the ball.

Make sure the grips of your clubs are kept clean. If they aren't then your hold on the club will be affected. When storing your clubs, be careful where you put them. Don't leave them in a position where other heavy articles can be piled on top of them. And if you leave your clubs in the boot of your car make sure they have plenty of room and are not crammed in, causing the shafts to bend.

95

· · · ·

GOLF BALLS

· · · ·

You will have noticed that all golf balls, apart from having the name of the manufacturer on them, also have a number for identification purposes, to enable players to spot their own ball quickly.

Many players believe that the higher the number, the better the ball. This is a complete fallacy. But if your mind tells you that you play better with a No.4 then by all means use a No.4 . . . after all, a lot of golf is played in the mind.

You'd be surprised how many matches start without players consulting each other about the type or number of ball being used. When two players go looking for lost balls they'll both discover they're using the same make and number of ball! So, consult with your partner or opponents before each round. However, two players can play with the same make of ball, and indeed same number, provided one, or both, marks the ball with a pen. Most professionals will mark a ball with their own characteristic marking by filling in a dimple or dimples.

96

· · · ·

CLOTHING

· · · ·

Golfing etiquette and rules must be obeyed at all times. And in particular rules about dress must be strictly adhered to, both on the course and in the clubhouse.

Most courses will not allow the wearing of jeans and certainly not track shoes. Shorts are also outlawed by many clubs in warm weather, but others are relaxing their rules on this subject and if, like Brian Barnes, you are more relaxed wearing shorts in warm weather, then check the local rules before you play.

In the clubhouse you may be requested to wear a tie and/or a jacket, so, if you want to enjoy the hospitality of the 19th after your round of golf, make sure you have both with you.

ABOVE The Balata ball has a rubber centre which is filled with water before rubber bands are wound around it

BELOW The Surlyn covered ball with a solid rubber centre

The beauty of the golf courses themselves is part of the attraction of the game

97

JOINING A GOLF CLUB

Joining a golf club is often a lengthy process. You normally have to be recommended and seconded for membership but in many cases waiting for a vacancy takes a long time.

If you want to join a club you are well advised to put your name forward as early as possibly and then be patient. You can, of course, in the meantime, play your golf on municipal courses or can play as a visitor at a private club.

98

BELIEVE IN YOURSELF

Quite often you will be faced with a shot and secretly tell yourself you can't play the shot. This lack of self-confidence will probably then tell in the shot and you *won't* play it. But if you have done everything right, and selected the right club, then there is no reason why you shouldn't be able to play the shot confronting you – unless you are being over-ambitious of course!

So, believe in yourself. And the more often you successfully make those seemingly 'impossible' shots, the better you will become. *Then* you can become more ambitious.

99

KEEP A DIARY

Most golfers with handicaps in excess of 20 probably play golf once a week, at the most. They will pack their clubs in their car, spend three and a half or four hours enjoying the round and forget all about it until the next time.

But if you want to improve your game and see where you are (or are not) making progress, you are well advised to keep a diary of all your rounds. Make a note of not only your scores, but how many greens you hit in regulation (don't forget you should hit a par three in one shot, a par four in two, and a par five in three shots), and how many fairways you hit off the tee. Also, make a note of how many putts you take on each hole.

It is a good idea to split every round you play into three parts, each lasting six holes. Aim for a score of 30 on each six and if, say, you shoot a 32 on the first six holes, then aim for a 28 on the next six in order to pull back those lost strokes. However, if you score 28 on the first six don't think you can ease off and aim for 32 on the next . . . try and shoot another 28. After a few weeks, analyze that lot and you will clearly see what kind of progress (or otherwise) you are making.

100

. . . .

NEVER BE AFRAID TO APPROACH A GOLF PROFESSIONAL

. . . .

Golfers who know go to their pro

PGA Professionals are not here just to run their pro shops or give golf lessons. They are here to offer advice to the golfing public. Don't be afraid to approach your PGA professional, he will be only too pleased to help in any way he can. You don't even have to be a member of a club to seek advice and help from a professional.

Professionals sell a wide range of golfing equipment, and will give you the correct advice on purchases. Many newcomers will often buy a set, or half set, of clubs by mail order and expect the clubs to be suitable for them. Your own individual make-up dictates the clubs you should buy, and only professional advice can guide you on this matter.

Regarding advice on golf techniques, all golfers should at some stage of their development seek advice from a professional who can instantly see what you are doing wrong and can help rectify your faults. Even if you have been playing golf for a few years, it never does any harm to return to your professional for a refresher course.

So, don't be afraid to approach your professional. He's a nice friendly guy and he has the interest of the game of golf and its players at heart. You cannot go to any better person for advice about the sport.

INDEX